ALL ABOUT INSECTS

ALL ABOUT MOTHS

by Golriz Golkar

pogo

Ideas for Parents and Teachers

Pogo Books let children practice reading informational text while introducing them to nonfiction features such as headings, labels, sidebars, maps, and diagrams, as well as a table of contents, glossary, and index.

Carefully leveled text with a strong photo match offers early fluent readers the support they need to succeed.

Before Reading

- "Walk" through the book and point out the various nonfiction features. Ask the student what purpose each feature serves.
- Look at the glossary together. Read and discuss the words.

Read the Book

- Have the child read the book independently.
- Invite him or her to list questions that arise from reading.

After Reading

- Discuss the child's questions. Talk about how he or she might find answers to those questions.
- Prompt the child to think more. Ask: Have you ever seen a moth? What color were its wings?

Pogo Books are published by Jump!
5357 Penn Avenue South
Minneapolis, MN 55419
www.jumplibrary.com

Library of Congress Cataloging-in-Publication Data

Names: Golkar, Golriz, author.
Title: All about moths / by Golriz Golkar.
Description: Minneapolis, MN: Jump!, Inc., [2025]
Series: All about insects | Includes index.
Audience: Ages 7-10
Identifiers: LCCN 2023052864 (print)
LCCN 2023052865 (ebook)
ISBN 9798889969938 (hardcover)
ISBN 9798889969945 (paperback)
ISBN 9798889969952 (ebook)
Subjects: LCSH: Moths–Juvenile literature.
Classification: LCC QL544.2 .G654 2025(print)
LCC QL544.2 (ebook)
DDC 595.78–dc23/eng/20231213
LC record available at https://lccn.loc.gov/2023052864
LC ebook record available at https://lccn.loc.gov/2023052865

Editor: Katie Chanez
Designer: Emma Almgren-Bersie

Photo Credits: Cathy Keifer/Shutterstock, cover; Jim and Lynne Weber/Shutterstock, 1; Eric Isselee/Shutterstock, 3; CathyKeifer/iStock, 4, 6-7; Hank Asia/Shutterstock, 5; Protasov AN/Shutterstock, 8; Richard Becker/Alamy, 9; www.pqpictures.co.uk/Alamy, 10-11; Sunshower Shots/Shutterstock, 12-13; Skip Moody/Dembinsky Photo Associates/Alamy, 14-15; Ian_Redding/iStock, 16; Heather Broccard-Bell/iStock, 17; Nikolay Kurzenko/Shutterstock, 18-19; kunakos/iStock, 20-21; Lux_D/iStock, 23.

Printed in the United States of America at Corporate Graphics in North Mankato, Minnesota.

TABLE OF CONTENTS

CHAPTER 1

HELLO, MOTH!

A fuzzy **insect** rests on a log. It has brown wings. They are covered in tiny **scales**. Two feathery **antennas** help the insect smell. It looks like a butterfly. But is it? No! It is a moth!

Moths are **related** to butterflies. There are around 160,000 moth **species**. Most are nocturnal. This means they are active at night.

Moths come in many sizes and colors. Some are bright. Others are dull. They blend in. Most have four wings to help them fly.

TAKE A LOOK!

What are the parts of a moth? Take a look!

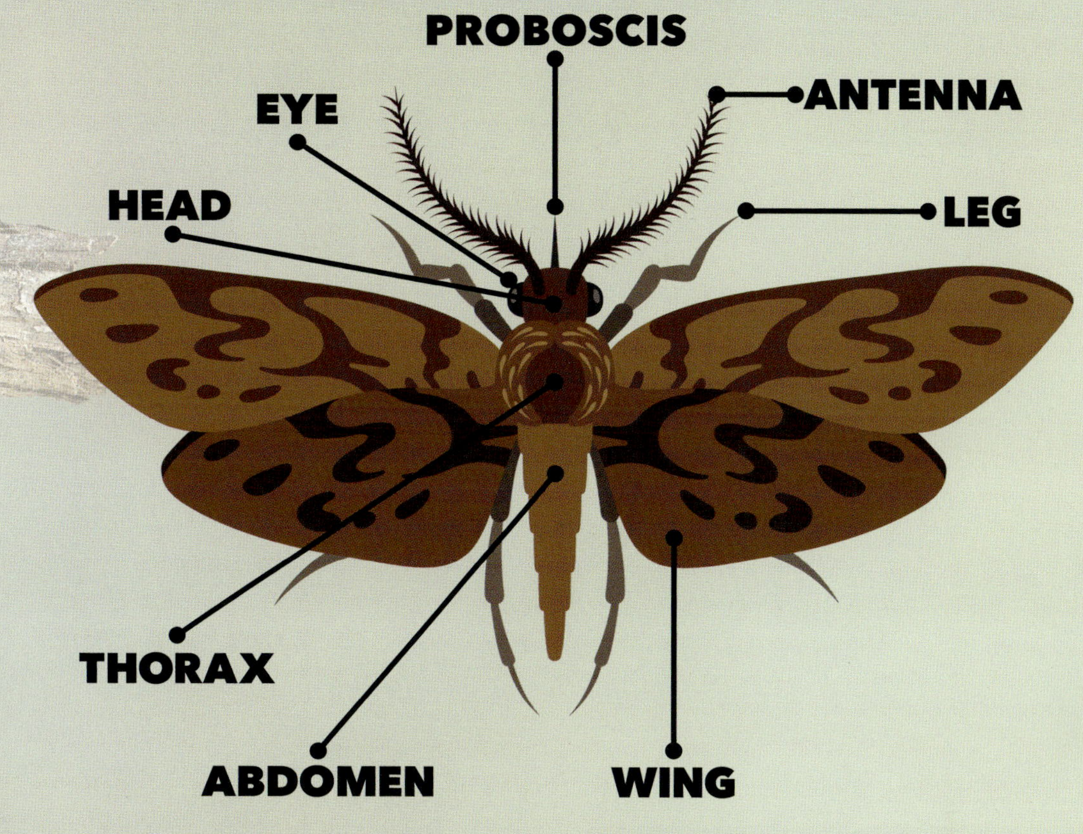

CHAPTER 2

LIFE CYCLE

Moths start life as eggs. Females lay hundreds of eggs on plants.

Larvae hatch from the eggs after one or two weeks. Moth larvae are also called caterpillars.

Larvae eat lots of plants.
They grow and **molt** many times.
They change colors and patterns.

DID YOU KNOW?

Moth larvae eat more than plants. Many eat clothes! They even eat rugs, blankets, and furniture. Cleaning and packing clothes can keep them away.

cocoon

After a few weeks, some larvae go underground. They grow hard skin cases. Others stick to plants. They spin **cocoons**. They become **pupae**. Inside, their bodies change.

When a pupa is done growing, its case or cocoon opens. An adult moth crawls out. Its wings dry. It flies away. It is time to **mate**. Antennas help moths smell mates. Males smell females from miles away!

TAKE A LOOK!

Moths grow in four stages. Take a look!

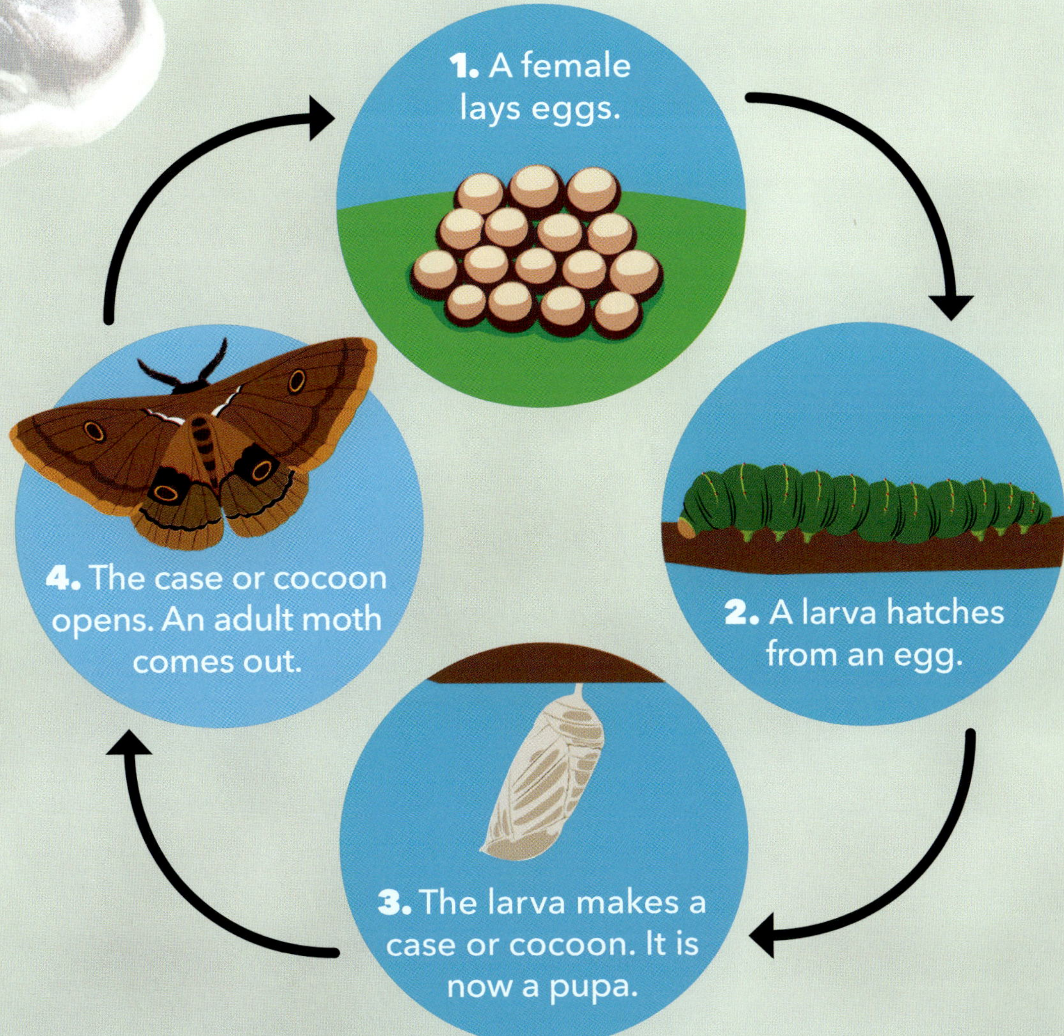

CHAPTER 3

MUNCHING MOTHS

Moths are **prey** for frogs, lizards, birds, and other small animals. Some moths have **camouflage**. This keeps them safe.

Some adult moths drink **nectar** through a **proboscis**. They spread pollen from plant to plant. Pollen helps plants make seeds. Moths are important **pollinators**.

luna moth

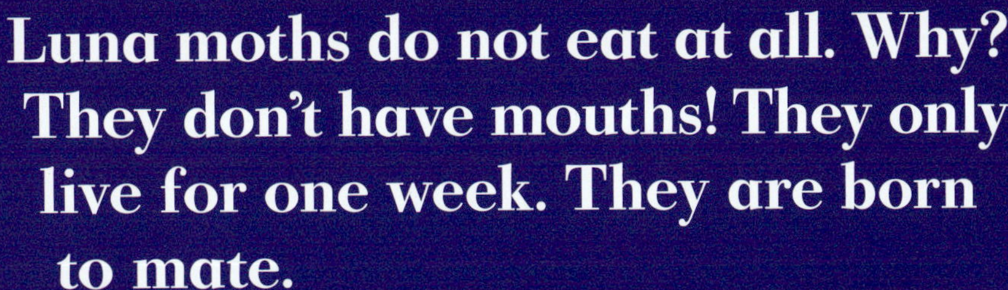

Luna moths do not eat at all. Why? They don't have mouths! They only live for one week. They are born to mate.

DID YOU KNOW?

Luna moths are some of North America's largest moths. They can be up to 5 inches (12.7 centimeters) long from wing to wing!

Moths need moonlight. Why? It helps them see at night. They find food or mates. Sometimes they fly to lamps and light bulbs. Have you ever seen a moth?

ACTIVITIES & TOOLS

TRY THIS!

POLLINATOR FOOD

Moths are important pollinators. Grow food for them in this fun activity!

What You Need:

- computer or other research device
- empty cardboard egg carton
- scissors
- metal or plastic tray
- potting soil
- native flower seeds
- water

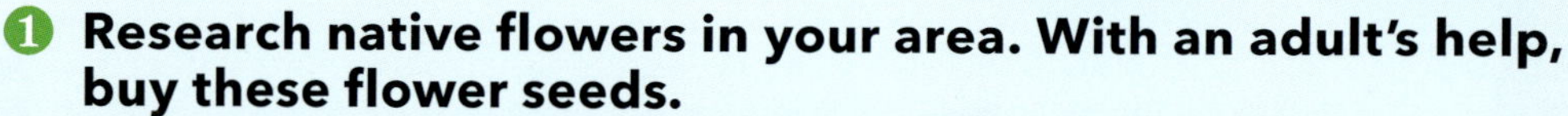

1. **Research native flowers in your area. With an adult's help, buy these flower seeds.**
2. **Cut off the top half of the egg carton. Then poke a hole in the bottom of each egg cup.**
3. **Set the carton in the tray. Fill each cup with potting soil.**
4. **Place a flower seed in each cup. Cover each seed with soil.**
5. **Pour a little water into each cup.**
6. **Place the tray in a sunny spot.**
7. **Watch your flowers. If the soil gets dry, add a little more water.**
8. **When the flowers sprout, cut the cups apart. Plant some outside. See what pollinators come to visit! Do you see any moths?**

GLOSSARY

antennas: Feelers on the head of an insect.

camouflage: A disguise or natural coloring that allows animals to hide by making them look like their surroundings.

cocoons: Covers made by young moths for protection as they change into adults.

insect: A small animal with three pairs of legs, one or two pairs of wings, and three main body parts.

larvae: Insects in the stage of growth between eggs and pupae.

mate: To come together to produce babies.

molt: To shed an old, outer skin so that a new one can grow.

nectar: A sweet liquid made by flowers.

pollinators: Animals and insects that carry pollen from flower to flower, allowing plants to form seeds.

prey: Animals that are hunted by other animals for food.

proboscis: A long, tubelike mouthpart that helps moths suck up liquids.

pupae: Insects in the stage of growth between larvae and adults.

related: Having a close connection.

scales: Thin, flat, overlapping pieces.

species: One of the groups into which similar animals and plants are divided.

INDEX

TO LEARN MORE

Finding more information is as easy as 1, 2, 3.

1. Go to www.factsurfer.com
2. Enter "moths" into the search box.
3. Choose your book to see a list of websites.